THE END OF A RAINBOW

Phil Hill

Jem Stone Publications

– Phil Hill

The End of a Rainbow – Complete Edition

A collection of heart-felt poems written by an expressive writer with lived experience, reflecting an inner desire for the reader's better understanding of the complexity of the human mind. The intention is clear - reaching the hearts of many by transcribing thoughts into verse that helps to heal people from trauma. Giving hope, understanding and insight into keeping the faith, holding a strong belief in recovery thus allowing others to learn from the challenges of another who has gone through difficult times, only to find adaptive ways of coping.

Jem Stone Publications

F o r e w o r d

The End of a Rainbow

This book is a collection of poetry about what it is to either find or lose hope. We are living, breathing beings that find and lose hope on our journeys. Many personal poems written in a more generic form than my last book

'Love/Resistance/Rebellion'

The rainbow is often a symbol of hope but appears fleetingly in our lives and it is in such moments that we discover meaning, purpose or in dark times; a reason to go on.

Hope is a very important metaphor in those who have experienced trauma and those who have become involved with the mental health system.

This book is by an author who has experienced severe mental illness and who has an ability and insight to reflect on his past despite the enduring side effects of his medication, which both control the illness and impede some of his thinking abilities to a small extent.

Phil Hill

Contents

Forward?

My boy-hood view

Of that concrete kingdom

That big, brash and bold
Centrally heated shopping mall

The way ahead they said

Even I could see that Godzilla
Standing statuesque

At its core surrounded by that
Token grassy lawn

A rotund towering building
I couldn't see the top of

As the sun streamed
And obscured viewing

Even then I could see the mildew

On that concrete

And within thirty years
Stripped down in its entirety

Thirty years later

And out of the demolition

Bold blue-painted concrete

Mollusc-like shell surrounded by
"A" complex of glass and steel

Twenty years had gone

And even I could see the glass

Wearing and the giant cd-like discs falling

From that mollusc-shape and that complex
Surrounding a defiant solitary old spire

A church that had stood and a community
That had worshiped a thousand years

The mildew now replaced the black soot

Rebuilt from the demolition of that war

From which a city, re-born for the car
And what buildings the blitz didn't destroy

That had blocked the Queensway
Being torn down

The way ahead they said

And many years later,
The roads paved over
As the car access depleted
And the pedestrian became king

The way ahead they said

And from before I was born
The tramways

Had snaked across the city
Replaced by buses and rebuilt much later
At much greater cost

The way ahead they said

Beauty in a Pink-Coat

Cherubic – your sculpted face
As it smiles at mine

Carefree – your locks of long, flowing hair
As you toss it from side to side

Inviting is your dis-arming voice

As it invites me in

Friendly are your eyes
As they stare at mine with interest

Subtle are your freckles
As they blend in with your complexion

Petite is your stature
As you look upwards at me

Pink is your coat shielding you as the
snow falls and you prevail

Transformed is your gaze
As you shut the door on me

Jesus Visiting an Asylum

'You didn't die for me, did you?'

A uniformed nurse said

'You gave your life away
Accepted that cup of suffering and strife'

'Not mine but your will', you said

'Sweated blood and tears
That rolled down your head'

'In that garden at Gethsemane
They then nailed you
To a cross-shaped tree'

'You didn't die for me, did you?'

Another voice said

'In my prophetic breakdown'

'Pharmacological treatment
Where the tablets swirled down'

'Not even you endured that
In your thorny crown'

'Or gave out an odour borne smell
In that chemical hell'

'You didn't die for me, did you?'

A bearded man shouted

'Or for those whose careers that failed'

'At that heir - very start'

'Or prevent those affairs of the heart'

'With altar-borne Commitment'

'Till death do us part'

'You didn't die for me, did you?'

A boy-like voice cried

'Or stop my suffering?'

'Or prevent me from regressing?'

'To a child in a man-hood form'

'You didn't calm that storm
Or build me back straight-away'

'I couldn't even tell night from day'

In reply, the white-robed person said

'But though'

'I Rose on that triumphant dawn
My shroud was all but torn'

'I couldn't prevent the weeping
Until like so many called by name'

'I put an end to shame'

'I was recognised then in the bread I broke'

My familiar voice spoke

'To Galilee, I went ahead'
'To trail a blaze for others no longer dead
They gladly took up their crosses instead'

'I rose for those
Who hung up a knotted rope
Their journey continued in hope'

'I rose for those
Who quit the drugs and drink
And helped them clear up their stink'

'And in the breaking of the bread
Outpouring of blood
Atoned for all sin instead'

'To rise, I had to die first'

'To save us all,
From unacknowledged
And sin unforgiven'

'I died to save you all
That's a given'

Social Distancing

Could you bear your own company
For what seems an eternity?

Or walk two-metres
Abreast of someone
In the street?

Or sacrifice a visit to your brother?
On his big day during the lock down?

And can you completely distance?
When falling completely in love?

Or can you restrain yourself?
When the phone becomes
A tool of incrimination?

Your motives lose transparency

And even when she finds you attractive
She may well be turned away

By your obsession,
Desperation and insecurity

Unsure in your own skin
Paranoid about losing face

Petrified of self-fulfilling nature
Of total rejection

From the very soulful entity he loves
Unable to retreat from the cul-de-sac

That buries you

When she joins those dots
Or spells things out

Can you accept the loss
Of the very person you truly loved?

In Sickness and in Health - 'Till Death Do Us Part

You made me feel needed
In the end
At the end
That look that said
I'm in extreme pain
And I trust you

You let me do my best
To reassure you

For those ever-lasting

Minutes you suffered
We waited and waited

Your look of affection

Then the nurses arrived
To administer the drug
That would comfort

Yet slowly suppress
Your breathing

You drifted into
A state of

Lesser consciousness

But not before you
Reached your hand

And we held together
Like we had for so long

I held you as long as
I could but

Death did part us

Though your sickness

Bound us for so long

In the beginning to

The very end

God Came to Leamington Spa

God came to Leamington Spa
But no-one seemed to listen

Or even see him from afar
And there was no sign
Of that wandering star

Was it that man in the retro car?
Or as tradition suggests

A guy in dirty swaddling sheets?
Yet to proclaim his mission

And yet there were no proclamations
To make converts of all nations

Or a Donkey in our line of vision?
Yet alone, palm leaves on the parade

Where it had been ridden
Or a thronging hoard
Outside the town hall?

To insist on crucifixion

But

Surely there were his friends

Who had left a legacy?

A long walk spoiled revealingly
In the breaking of communion wafers

Wine to be had at that wedding
Without hesitancy

Or was it the priest?
Who from the pulpit

Did not waver?

Or was it the talk
Of the meaning of life?
At that house called the 'Fat Pug'

To a person struggling
As sworn
Enemies forgive and hug

To those who have ears
Let them hear

A story of a town called Leamington
Where lives are transformed

One at a time
A facet of heaven

If I Knew Then

If I knew then
How messed up
You can be

Would I dare to dream?

Would I have passed
Any induction probation?

And what not

Would I have just stood there
And then given up?

Any type of hope

Yet, alone
A lone worker
A Career
If I knew then
How painful
Life can be

How much
Rejection
Would hurt

Demotion, humiliation

And such like

Would I have dared
To dream?

Would I have found space for?

The possible
Amongst the Impossible?

If I knew then
How much I would learn

How much I would fight
How much I would pick

And scrape myself
Off of the floor
And carry on

Would I have delayed
That ambition?

If I knew then
How partially formed I was

Would I have really believed
I could be where I am now?

If I understood then
How dashed my dreams became

Would I dare to believe
I could arrive
At any type of peace

But I didn't understand

My dreams were dashed
My world would be judged
My very soul would be damaged

But not beyond repair
Or transformation

I could never have
Followed my dreams

Then I didn't reach the mountain top
But in the landscape of life

At a different peak
I live another dream

At the end of
Another rainbow

But don't stop dreaming
Don't close off possibilities

But don't let dreams
Be your master

To block out other journeys
When the fork in the road appears

Bees, Wasps and Humans

Friends yell as they often do

Duck heads and swipe
With newspapers and magazines
"Aren't wasps, creatures
Whom sting without conscience?"

"Unlike the humble bee who stings
To defend and yet die on their own sword"

Replying in kind
The supreme voice had choice words

"Humankind is both the bee
And the wasp"

"Stinging the earth and its creation
Without conscience"

"And even in that ethical shift
Humankind merely manages their own
Extinction in the act of inflicting pain
On the few that will remain

Belonging?

In that primordial melting-pot, I grew?
In that Euro-centric
Mono culture?

The so-called dominant
Culture, race and
Gender?

The years that passed
Still at the apex?

With each decade a new frontier?

Of those forging
Through those

Ceilings to sit alongside?

In that modern cauldron Equality?
Does that come from Diversity?

No longer perceived as dominant

But

Christian, White and Male.

But in that city, I lived

New frontiers emerge

Can I be my own creation?
And affiliate as I please?

Will I be accepted?
With any kind of ease?

With which group can I identify?

Which struggle must I fight?

To whom do I truly belong?
Can they accept my own creation?
And can I be the real me?

The End of a Rainbow

A small gate
Lay open on the horizon

Beyond which, the sun
Rose like a new dawn

Venturing forward
The path narrowed

Approaching the gate
The path fell away at both sides

Leaving a jutting ridge

The path had been wider

From far out

But as the walk progressed
It had converged

Not only this
But what remained

Was a poor excuse
For what had been a road

Which wound one way

Then the other

But

Always, always the gate
Remained in sight

Finally reaching my goal
I walked through

The light intensified
My companion

Seemed to glow so brightly
In a way that was beyond words

I could smell the fragrance of flowers
Never before encountered

At the same time, it seemed
Overwhelming

And elevated in mood

There was a sudden realisation
An awareness of peace

Forgiveness and love intermingled

The clouds, which had hovered, lifted

In front of me was a panoramic view

I noticed the scenes of all that had
Gone before in a flash

Below I could see the hospital bed and
Loved ones crying, hugging each other

Then the coffin

After which, I began to realise

The seeds I had sown, had grown

Nieces and nephews got married

Starting new careers

Living on in lives of those

I had touched

Then the crowds

Waiting

Of everyone I had ever met

Smiling, shaking hands, one at a time

For all the years of searching

I had finally arrived

The Boxer

Always punching above their weight
The fighter had gone from strength
To strength

From challenge after challenge
But they had always so

Not understanding how uneven the ground
On which they stood

Not grasping the power of the unsaid
Not taking in the whole view

From another advantage point
The partiality of their progress

Their profile jagged with
Incredible peaks

Unsupported troughs

On a fragile foundation stone
How strong they could seem to be

The vulnerability being the other side
Of that coin

They had never escaped the Gaze

Of the critical parental bird

On their shoulder

And how on occasions they couldn't throw
That punch and could not duck

The approaching jab
Their demeanour frozen

Taking the full force of that jab
Fate had caught up with him

Parent on my shoulder

The voice that drives him on and on
Drowning out that space

Room to think?

The pretence of a smile.
Is everything ok?

Flat out and on and on he must go

Can he stop that treadmill?
Or fall from the blow of exhaustion

And disintegration

Will he ever discover the cognitive secret?

Too much drive
Too much sloth

Too much trauma

Concentration hanging by a thread

Tablets that alert the brain
Tablets that slow thinking pressure

Unfathomably
The cognitive conundrum

Ludwig's Nightmare

He can't mime
Or recite that tune

Heard at the end of that film

The shop assistant is stunned
As his irrepressible customer

Hums the melody

With another so-called tune

He thinks his luck betwixt
'It's symphony number 9'

Or is it number six?

I'm not sure

What do you think?

'It's definitely Number 6.'
He replied

Alas
Poor Ludwig
Would turn in his grave

And tell this man
To behave

To hear his music quoted out of
Context, pitch or rhythm

Money's saved to
Spend on recordings

By his hometown band

With a mere paltry
String and chorale settings
To drums and lead guitar

Thinking himself, street cred
To broadcast such music to

Outside his head

To any neighbour who would listen
Thinking that people
Appreciate poor Ludwig on

Repeat

The romantic 'Scene by the brook'

Interspersed by in that summer heat

With 'musical thunder and lightning'

Then the shepherd's song brings

Light relief to everyone

Before the academic term
Has gone

Alas

Poor Ludwig
Had thought he was

Careful

What he wished for
With final words

'I'll hear in heaven'

Lockdown
– I am anyone

An infection

I am anyone who

Can die

I am an absence

Of presence

A yearning
Of Feeling

Untouched

A connection with

Distant people

Yet,

A 2-metre disconnect from

Everything

My mask, my gloves, my apron, my
visor

Barriers

Are you a carrier?

Am I a carrier?

Are we carriers?

I am everyone and everyone is anyone.

Clinging on

Over the decade that had passed

My family members now few in number
Had each individually departed

When you hold each weak skinny hand
And make that brief connection

As you become aware of mortality

They just want to know they
Are loved and cherished

And that somehow...somehow
Their lives had mattered

They smile in recognition of love given
You smile because it's all you have to give.

Such depletion
Makes each new encounter
Each conversation so much more

Telling on, when the time comes
On our remembrance

Those that died and mattered
Leave an imprint

On our hearts

And in that way
They live on

In all of us

Labour of Love

Not coping with the idea of love

Overqualified in everything else

Not translating their language

But clued up on chat-up lines

Jokes and small talk

Not sensing their occasional

Interest until I commit everything

On then shifting sands of feelings

Changed

Unable to process rejection to become

Overqualified in self-loathing

What is it to really love?

What qualities do I need?

Will it do to wait and will someone really

Like my bad as well as my good-self?

Will the anchor of love firmly find?

It's place amongst the rocky shores?

Will I ever truly feel free?

And when will I not take notice of

Everyone except sometimes me?

Yellow Gaze

Couldn't bring
Myself to tell you

The tinge your face
Had turned

A twenty-year marriage
Left me thinking

I had earned the right
To tell you

More than about
The weather outside

Celebrity gossip
The TV programme on
The other side

Sitting near
Still unwell

Exhausted

Despite
The ten-week lie-in

But

Only I knew
The real you

Now

And it wasn't just
A bout of flu

Something profound
Was wrong with you

Then

I told you the tinge
Your face and skin had
Turned

And
Into the face mirror
You looked

Screaming denial
Then anger

Alongside each other
We cried

There was no more place
For you to hide

You had resisted

Time and again

My invitation to the
Medical gaze

To avoid the diagnosis
Of the coming pain

The phone rang

Your voice so serene
At the other end

You did not intend
To draw the shutter

On my small world

In sickness and in health
'Till death do us part

I said I would be with you
Till the bitter end

Those spots on your liver
Would grow and
Never disappear

I told you
I would always be near

At the foot of the stairs
You had fallen

The ambulance lost
But on its way

And after, settling
On the hospital trolley

You said

All the things
You wanted

At the very end

The hymns
The poetry
And the fact

Your life
Had to
Have a positive

Commentary

To this, I promised
I would tend

The desperate look
Of a gaze wracked with pain

Shouting the nurse

As the morphine
Drivers

Pumped in vain

That ten-minute
Wait was eternity

Comforting worst
Recite time and again

In mellow mantra
Till nurses arrive

To temper the pain

Your arm strayed
Upwards in the air

As the medic says she wants to
Hold you now

And grasping your hands
As I did, I bid farewell

But held you 'till the very end

I had worn that t-shirt
'Till death do us part'

To the very

End

Today to your memory
I tend

Living on in me

Not written in ink

On cotton worn

On the chest

But written on my heart

So, you can now rest.

In Peace

Doctor in the Family

He'd been stacking shelves
And hit that transparent ceiling

In a moment realisation projecting
To the perpetual Groundhog Day

He could see in that moment
Years ahead and the futility of it all

Absconding secretly to
Develop skills that had been

Hidden his powers had been
Dormant but the

Deep thaw made sure
They rose to the surface

Fear drove him

Failure... failure

He couldn't
Face yet driving himself into a frenzy
His companion kept
Him well

And a six-year writing stint
Punctuated by assessment of
Every kind and viewed by that
Community from all angles.

Managing himself to be
Free from reproach

He had written
Read and presented himself

Constantly refining his expertise
Until that day when

Given those keys by his
Peers to the community of learning

Reaching the apex of that Maslow like
Pyramid beyond fulfilment

He could now blaze a trail for himself
And others

Whilst nurturing the next generation
He had become the
Doctor of all he surveyed

The Gospel According to the White Van Man

White van man is to be found across the land
As many as grains on a beach of sand

'Did you hear?'
'Did you hear?'
A white van man said

As the blood of anger rushed to his head

He stood a big-built figure
With coffee stains on his newspaper

The belt he wears holds it in
That face had long since, lost its grin
'They come here'
'They come here'
'Get council house, NHS'
'Benefits, the lot'

'That's a pretty dawn site'
'More than I've got'

'You pay your taxes, rent
For all those years'

'Working all hours, God sends'

'It's enough to drive you round the bend'

Paper in hand, unfurled
He puffs and grinds and reads
From the sixty-font print
As if from the pulpit
You couldn't make up this shit

Context irrelevant,
The case study that proves the rule
He will tell you, he's nobody's fool
Then he and his apprentice trade more facts

The HR Managers
Had better not catch them in the act
Tabloid statements from on high
The drivers think
They're modern types of guy
Bring back hanging or even the birch

And resurrect the stop and search

Across the country,
White van men seek to serve

The country gets
The government it deserves

Recommendation

Having known Philip since 2012, I consider him to be a friend, confidante, trustworthy soul-mate who I can relate to and understand, having empathy for his past experiences. I have become a person who has facilitated and fine-tuned his expression of his poetry, having felt no reason to alter the way he projects his thoughts onto paper. Despite the illness he has been diagnosed, Philip writes with such clarity, realism and with a huge understanding of humanity, expressing himself in an honest, sincere and insightful way to expose his most internal directional thoughts to the reader, connecting common human experiences on a deeper level.

Jemma Stone

Educationalist, Mentor, Friend, Typist, Proof-Reader

Read more of Philip Hill's poetry with expressive insights into his life experiences in Love/Resistance/Rebellion and Beyond the Wilderness. Discover what people have said about these poetry books. Available on ebook and paperback. Books in both formats can be purchased from

www.philhillpoetry.co.uk www.philhillpoetry.com
www.deloragreen.org.uk www.jemmastone.org

Testimonial 1

Philip Hill's powerful new collection does not flinch from exploring some of the key dilemmas that ultimately confront us all. What might it mean to acknowledge and recognize our pasts and ourselves; to forgive and to seek forgiveness; to be reconciled without deformity; and to discover – and speak boldly from – that place of integrity which is to be found in the deepest recesses of our being?

This is poetry to be spoken aloud and wondered at. It both consoles and challenges with its blend of tenderness, raw honesty and hard-won wisdom. Nourishment from a poet rich in maturity of voice and vision.

Fiona Breckenridge.

Former Student of English, Mentor, Friend.

Testimonial 2

Poetry is a condensed and direct form of words that speaks to a variety of human situations but it is especially suited to exploring the intricacies of human relationships, the accompanying emotions, the unspoken angst, and the unspeakable terror of rejection. Philip Hill, in these poems, has worked the magic of words, that combination of precise diction and euphony, that speak directly to the heart. I feel very honoured to have been asked to write a foreword for this collection of poetry. I have been moved and touched, and also changed. That, in the end is what poetry aims at.

Professor Femi Oybode.

Professor of Psychiatry, University of Birmingham, Poet.